MONKEYS OF ASIA AND AFRICA

A TRUE BOOK

by

Patricia A. Fink Martin

Children's Press®
A Division of Grolier Publishing

New York London Hong Kong Sydney
Danbury, Connecticut

Male mandrills have a brightly colored face.

Reading Consultant
Linda Cornwell
*Coordinator of School Quality
and Professional Improvement
Indiana State Teachers Association*

Content Consultant
Kathy Carlstead, Ph.D.
*National Zoological Park
Washington, D.C.*

The photograph on the cover shows a baboon. The photograph on the title page shows two patas monkeys.

Visit Children's Press® on the Internet at:
http://publishing.grolier.com

Library of Congress Cataloging-in-Publication Data

Martin, Patricia A. Fink, 1955–
    Monkeys of Asia and Africa / by Patricia A. Fink Martin.
        p. cm. — (A true book)
    Includes bibliographical references and index.
    Summary: Describes the physical characteristics, habitats, life cycles, and behavior of Old World monkeys, which live in Asia and Africa.
    ISBN: 0-516-21573-6 (lib. bdg.)   0-516-27016-8 (pbk.)
    1. Cebidae—Juvenile literature. [1. Monkeys.] I. Title. II. Series.
QL737.P63M375 2000
599.8'6'095—dc21
                                                                99-17064
                                                                    CIP
                                                                     AC

Contents

If you drew a monkey,
would it look like this?

What Is a Monkey?

Can you draw a picture of a monkey? If you could, what would it look like? Would your drawing show an animal with brown fur and a long tail? Would the monkey be climbing a tree or swinging from a branch? Would it live in the jungle?

Japanese macaques live high in the mountains of Japan (right). Celebes macaques have dark fur and black faces (middle). Proboscis monkeys have brown heads and silver bodies (bottom).

That type of drawing would show what some kinds of monkeys are like. But there are many kinds of monkeys. Some monkeys have brown fur. But others have orange, red, white, or yellow coats.

Only a few monkeys swing from tree branches. They have special tails that can grasp onto things. Most run along tree branches on all fours. Not all monkeys live in the jungle. Some live in grasslands or high in the mountains.

Monkeys are a type of mammal. Scientists place them in a group of mammals called primates. Chimpanzees and lemurs are primates too, and so are humans. Primates are smart animals with large brains. They have eyes in the front of their heads. This helps them to know whether the objects they see are near-by or far away.

Like monkeys, chimpanzees (top) and lemurs (bottom) are primates.

This vervet monkey is using its fingers to peel fruit.

Monkeys have hands like yours. All primates—including humans—have hands made for grasping. They can use their fingers to pick up and hold objects. Monkeys use their hands to peel fruit or grab branches.

Our Hands Are Special

A dog's paw is very different from our hands. If you trace both, you will really be able to see the differences.

Compare your hands to the paws of a dog or a cat. If you know a calm, friendly dog, try this. Trace the outline of the dog's front paw on paper. Reach between each toe as you draw. Now trace your hand. How are the two tracings alike? How are they different? Can you think of other ways hands and paws are different?

This white-faced capuchin lives in Costa Rica. It can use its tail to grab tree branches.

Two Kinds of Monkeys

Scientists divide monkeys into two groups. One group lives in Central and South America. They can use their tails to grab onto tree branches.

The second group of monkeys is found in Africa and Asia. Most of them have narrow noses. They also have

These celebes crested macaques live in Indonesia.

hardened seat pads that protect their bottoms. Some of these monkeys have a long tail, and some have a short tail. Others have no tail at all.

Monkeys that live in Asia and Africa are called Old World monkeys. Many years ago, explorers from Europe sailed across the Atlantic Ocean and discovered the Americas. Because these lands were new to the explorers, the explorers called them

When European explorers arrived in America, they called this new land the New World.

the New World. They called the lands they already knew about (Europe, Asia, and Africa) the Old World.

Most people do not use these terms anymore. But scientists still name the two groups of monkeys in this way. They call them New World monkeys and Old World monkeys.

A proboscis monkey spends most of its time in trees.

The Proboscis Monkey

The proboscis monkey is a big orange and silver monkey. It lives on the island of Borneo in Southeast Asia. Proboscis monkeys are found in trees near rivers and in swamps. At night, they sleep in trees that hang over the

The proboscis monkey has a large belly.

water. There, they are safe from their enemies.

During the day, they feed on leaves. They have a big belly with an extra stomach pouch. Bacteria live in that pouch and help the monkeys digest leaves.

It is easy to tell male proboscis monkeys from females. Males are about twice as large as females. Their noses are larger too. The male's nose hangs below its mouth!

The male proboscis monkey (left) has a much larger nose than the female (right).

A mother proboscis monkey spends most of her time taking care of her young.

The female's nose is shaped like a beak.

Why do the males have such a long nose? No one knows for sure. Perhaps the females prefer mates with long noses. The shape of a male's nose does change the sound of its honking call.

Proboscis monkeys live in groups. The males defend the females and the young. They often scare away enemies with their loud honking.

The Hanuman Langur

The Hanuman langur is also a large monkey. But it does not have a potbelly like the proboscis monkey. The langur's body is long and lean. Its dark face, hands, and feet stand out against its silver fur. Its long tail curves up over its back.

The Hanuman languar has a long, lean body.

To some people, these monkeys are sacred. Hindus believe that the monkey god, Hanuman, and his troops fought evil monsters to save a goddess. Today these monkeys carry the god's name.

Six Hanuman langurs spend the afternoon on the roof of a building in Jodhpur, India.

You can find Hanuman langurs everywhere in India. They live in cities, small villages, and forests. They are at home on the ground and in the trees.

These monkeys spend most of their time in large groups

called troops. Many troops consist of several females, their young, and one adult male. This male mates with all the adult females in his troop. This type of troop is called a harem. If other males approach, fierce battles occur.

These Hanuman langurs are members of the same troop.

The Golden Monkey

Golden monkeys live in the mountain forests of China. In the summer, they feed high in the mountains. They like to eat young leaves from fir trees and pine trees. They also eat nuts, berries, and bark.

When winter comes, they migrate. They move down the

The golden monkey has
bright fur and a blue face.

mountains to the valleys. The
valleys are not quite as cold
as the mountaintops. Their
thick fur keeps golden monkeys warm.

A golden monkey's thick fur keeps it warm all winter.

Every fall, golden monkeys shed their old coat and grow long, heavy fur for the winter. To stay warm, males and females hold each other close. It looks like they are giving each other hugs!

The male's thick coat is the color of fire, and the female's is a more faded yellowish gold. At one time, these monkeys were hunted for their lovely fur. But today they are an endangered species. It is against the law to harm them.

Like most other monkeys, golden monkeys are members of a troop.

The Baboon

Bands of olive-gray baboons roam the African plains. They walk or run on all fours. They have a long snout, so they look a little like dogs. But their hands give them away. They use their long fingers to pluck tiny seeds from the grass.

This baboon family lives in a national park in Tanzania.

There are few trees on the African plains, so baboons cannot hide from their enemies. To protect themselves, baboons live in large troops. When one baboon spots an

Baboons are rarely found alone. They travel in large troops.

enemy, it warns the others— without making a sound. The baboon uses body language.

Many primates use their body and face to send signals. Even humans do this.

Can you make an angry face?
A scared face? A happy face?
See if you can send a mes-
sage without saying a word.

What do you think this
baboon is trying to say?

The Patas Monkey

The patas monkey, like the baboon, lives on the hot, dry African plains. There are few trees here, so this red-coated monkey spends most of its day moving across the plains. It has long legs, so it can run fast. Some patas monkeys can travel up to 35 miles (56 km)

Patas monkeys live in grasslands in Africa (above). This patas monkey has found a tasty flower (right).

per hour. When a patas monkey spots a tree, it climbs up and looks for fruits, leaves, and flowers to eat.

A male patas monkey is always on the lookout for enemies.

The male patas monkey is large. As the only adult male in a troop, his job is to stand guard. He protects the females and the young. When he spots danger, the male jumps up and down. He may also bark at the enemy so that the predator notices him before the others. The patas monkey then runs away at full speed. The enemy chases the male, so the rest of the troop is safe.

Monkeys in Many Places

Old World monkeys are a highly adaptable group of animals. They survive in many different places. Many make their homes in trees. Others prefer to live on the ground. Most live in forests, but some live in open grasslands.

Liontail macaques can be found in southwestern India.

Like other primates, Old World monkeys are in danger. Many are killed by hunters for their meat or their fur. Others are captured and kept as pets or sold to zoos. The monkeys that manage to avoid hunters have another problem. Their

The forests where many monkeys live are being cut down for wood and farming. Where will the monkeys go?

homes are being destroyed as people clear land for wood or for farming.

Many people want to help the monkeys. They are working hard to protect them. But that may not be enough. If the places where monkeys live are destroyed, they will not

These langurs live in a national park in Vietnam.

be able to survive. In some countries, national parks have been created to protect monkeys and their habitats. Only with our help will monkeys survive.

To Find Out More

If you would like to learn more about the monkeys from Asia and Africa, check out these additional resources.

 **Books**

Arnold, Caroline. **Monkey**. Morrow Junior Books, 1993.

Lemmon, Tess. **Wildlife at Risk**: Monkeys. Bookwright Press, 1992.

Maynard, Thane. **Primates: Apes, Monkeys, Prosimians.** Franklin Watts, 1994.

Rinard, Julie and National Geographic Staff. **National Geographic Amazing Monkeys.** National Geographic, 1994.

Steedman, Scott. **Amazing Monkeys.** Knopf Books for Young Readers, 1991.

Organizations and Online Sites

Hanuman Langur
*http://www.
birminghamzoo.com/ao/
mammal/hanlangr.htm*

This site features photographs and general information about Hanuman langurs.

International Primate Protection League
P.O. Box 766
Summerville, SC 29484
http://www.ippl.org

The Nature Conservancy
Adopt-an-Acre Program
1815 North Lynn Street
Arlington, VA 22209

Old World Monkeys
*http://www.oit.itd.umich.
edu/bio108/Chordata/
Mammalia/Primates/
Cercopithecidae.html*

Find out about macaques, rhesus monkeys, mangabeys, mandrills, guenons, patas monkeys, langurs, proboscis monkeys, colubus, and other Old World monkeys.

Rainforest Action Network
221 Pine Street, Suite 500
San Francisco, CA 94104
*http://www.ran.org/
kids_action/index.html*

Important Words

bacteria tiny, single-celled living things that can be seen only using a microscope

endangered species living things that are in danger of dying out

harem a social group of female animals and their children, controlled by one male

mammal an animal that has a backbone and fur, is warm-blooded, and produces milk for its young

migrate to move, usually as a group, from one place to another for purposes of mating or feeding

predator an animal that hunts another animal for food

primate a member of the group of mammals with eyes that face forward, hands that grasp, and a large brain

troop a small band or group of animals of the same kind that feed, sleep, and travel together

Index

Meet the Author

Patricia A. Fink Martin has a doctorate in biology. After working in the laboratory and teaching for 10 years, she began writing science books for children. *Booklist* chose her first book, *Animals that Walk on Water*, as one of the ten best animal books for children in 1998. Dr. Martin lives in Tennessee with her husband, Jerry, and their daughter, Leslie.